MW00564363

CUTE CROCHET Rugs FOR KIDS™

TARA COUSINS

Contents

Give a Hoot
OWL

SKILL LEVEL

◧■□□

EASY

FINISHED MEASUREMENTS

19 inches wide x 34 inches long

MATERIALS

- Deborah Norville Everyday Soft Worsted Solids medium (worsted) weight acrylic yarn (4 oz/203 yds/ 113g per skein):
    2 skeins #1035 cappuccino (A)
    1 skein each #1016 kiwi (B), #1001 snow white (C), #1028 mustard (D), #1011 chocolate (E) and #1022 bittersweet (F)
- Size M/N/13/9mm crochet hook or size needed to obtain gauge
- Size I/9/5.5mm crochet hook
- Tapestry needle

GAUGE

Size M/N hook and 2 strands of yarn held tog:
    9 sc and 10 rows = 4 inches

PATTERN NOTES

Weave in ends as work progresses.

Join with slip stitch as indicated unless otherwise stated.

Chain-2 at beginning of round counts as first double crochet unless otherwise stated.

SPECIAL STITCH

Long double crochet (long dc): Yo, insert hook from front to back in indicated st 2 rows below, pull up to height of working row, [yo, pull through 2 lps] twice.

BODY & HEAD

Row 1 (RS): With M/N hook and 2 strands of A held tog, ch 16, sc in 2nd ch from hook and in each rem ch across, turn. *(15 sc)*

Rows 2 & 3: Ch 1, 2 sc in first st, 2 sc in next st, sc in each st across to last 2 sts, [2 sc in next st] twice, turn. *(23 sc)*

Row 4: Ch 1, 2 sc in first st, sc in each st to last st, 2 sc in last st, turn. *(25 sc)*

Row 5: Ch 1, sc in each st across, turn.

Rows 6–8: Rep row 4. *(31 sc at end of last row)*

Rows 9 & 10: Ch 1, sc in each st across, turn.

Row 11: Rep row 4. *(33 sc)*

Rows 12–17: [Rep rows 9–11 consecutively] twice. *(37 sc at end of last row)*

Rows 18–21: Ch 1, sc in each st across, turn.

Row 22: Rep row 4. *(39 sc)*

Rows 23–41: Ch 1, sc in each st across, turn.

Row 42: Ch 1, **sc dec** *(see Stitch Guide)* in first 2 sts, sc in each st across to last 2 sts, sc dec in last 2 sts, turn. *(37 sc)*

Rows 43–45: Rep row 4.

Row 46: Rep row 42. *(35 sc)*

Rows 47 & 48: Ch 1, sc in each st across, turn.

Row 49: Rep row 42. *(33 sc)*

Row 50: Ch 1, sc in each st across, turn.

Row 51: Rep row 42. *(31 sc)*

Rows 52–54: Ch 1, sc in each st across, turn.

Row 55: Rep row 4. *(33 sc)*

Rows 56 & 57: Ch 1, sc in each st across, turn.

Rows 58–63: [Rep rows 55–57] twice. *(37 sc at end of last row)*

Rows 64–70: Ch 1, sc in each st across, turn.

Row 71: Rep row 42. *(35 sc)*

Row 72: Ch 1, sc in each st across, turn.

Rows 73–76: [Rep rows 71 and 72 alternately] twice. Do not fasten off. *(31 sc at end of last row)*

FIRST EAR

Row 1 (RS): Ch 1, sc in each of first 7 sts, sc dec in next 2 sts, leaving rem sts unworked, turn. *(8 sc)*

Row 2: Ch 1, sc dec in first 2 sts, sc in each rem st across, turn. *(7 sc)*

Row 3: Ch 1, sc in each of first 4 sc, sc dec in next 2 sts, leaving last st unworked, turn. *(5 sc)*

Row 4: Rep row 2. *(4 sc)*

Row 5: Ch 1, 2 sc in first st, sc in next st, sc dec in last 2 sts, turn. *(4 sc)*

Row 6: Ch 1, sc dec in first 2 sts, sc in each of last 2 sts. Fasten off. *(3 sc)*

2ND EAR

Row 1: With WS facing and 2 strands of A held tog, **join** *(see Pattern Notes)* in right-hand corner, ch 1, sc in each of first 7 sts, sc dec in next 2 sts, leaving rem sts unworked, turn. *(8 sc)*

Rows 2–6: Rep rows 2–6 of First Ear. At end of last row, do not fasten off.

BODY EDGING

With RS facing, ch 1, work sc evenly sp around outer edge, working 3 sc in corner of each Ear, join in first sc. Fasten off.

WING
Make 2.

Row 1 (RS): With I hook and B, ch 4, sc in 2nd ch from hook and in each of next 2 chs, turn. *(3 sc)*

Row 2: Ch 1, 2 sc in first st, sc in next st, 2 sc in last st, turn. *(5 sc)*

Row 3: Ch 1, 2 sc in first st, sc in each st across to last st, 2 sc in last st, turn. *(7 sc)*

Row 4: Ch 1, sc in first st, ***long dc** (see Special Stitch) in next st 2 rows below, sc in next st, rep from * across, turn.

Rows 5-10: [Rep rows 3 and 4 alternately] 3 times. *(13 sc at end of last row)*

Row 11: Ch 1, sc in each st across, turn.

Row 12: Ch 1, long dc in first st 2 rows below, *sc in next st, long dc in next st 2 rows below, rep from * across, turn.

Row 13: Rep row 11.

Row 14: Ch 1, sc in first st, *long dc in next st 2 rows below, sc in next st, rep from * across, turn.

Rows 15–50: [Rep rows 11–14 consecutively] 9 times.

Rows 51 & 52: Rep rows 11 and 12.

Row 53: Ch 1, sc dec in first 2 sts, sc in each st across to last 2 sts, sc dec in last 2 sts, turn. *(11 sc)*

Row 54: Ch 1, long dc in first st 2 rows below, *sc in next st, long dc in next st 2 rows below, rep from * across, turn.

Row 55: Ch 1, sc in each st across, turn.

Row 56: Ch 1, sc in first st, *long dc in next st 2 rows below, sc in next st, rep from * across, turn.

Row 57: Ch 1, sc dec in first 2 sts, sc in each st across to last 2 sts, sc dec in last 2 sts, turn. *(9 sc)*

Rows 58–63: [Rep rows 56 and 57 alternately] 3 times. *(3 sc at end of last row)*

WING EDGING
With WS facing, ch 1, work sc evenly sp around, join in first sc. Fasten off.

EYE
Make 2.

EYEBALL
Rnd 1 (RS): With I hook and C, ch 4, join in first ch to form ring, **ch 2** *(see Pattern Notes)*, 15 dc in ring, join in 2nd ch of beg ch-2. *(16 dc)*

Rnd 2: Ch 2, dc in first st, 2 dc in each rem st around, join in first st. *(32 dc)*

Rnd 3: Ch 2, dc in first st and in next st, *2 dc in next st, dc in next st, rep from * around, join in first st, **changing color** *(see Stitch Guide)* to E, turn. Fasten off C. *(48 dc)*

Rnd 4 (WS): Ch 1, sc in each st around, join in first st. Leaving long end for sewing, fasten off.

PUPIL
Rnd 1 (RS): With I hook and E, ch 4, join in first ch to form ring, ch 1, 7 sc in ring, join in first sc. *(7 sc)*

Rnd 2: Ch 1, 2 sc in each st around, join in first sc. Leaving long end for sewing, fasten off. *(14 sc)*

BEAK
With I hook and D, ch 8, sl st in 2nd ch from hook, sc in next ch, hdc in next ch, dc in next ch, tr in each of next 2 chs, **dtr** *(see Stitch Guide)* in last ch. Leaving long end for sewing, fasten off.

SPOT
Make 7.

With I hook and F, ch 4, join in first ch to form ring, ch 1, 7 sc in ring, join in first sc. Leaving long end for sewing, fasten off. *(7 sc)*

FOOT
Make 2.

With I hook and D, ch 16, dc in 3rd ch from hook, dc in each of next 4 chs, *sk next 2 chs, sl st in next ch, ch 7, sc in 3rd ch from hook and each of next 4 chs, rep from * once, sk next 2 chs, sl st in last ch. Leaving long end for sewing, fasten off.

FINISHING
Referring to photo for placement, with B and with RS facing, sew Wings to Body. Sew Pupils to Eyeballs. With WS facing, sew Feet to Body. With RS facing, sew Spots to Body. ■

Bella
BUTTERFLY

SKILL LEVEL

EASY

FINISHED MEASUREMENTS
32 inches wide x 30 inches long

MATERIALS

- Deborah Norville Everyday Soft Worsted Solids medium (worsted) weight acrylic yarn (4 oz/203 yds/113g per skein):
  - 3 skeins #1020 orchid (A)
  - 1 skein each #1010 aubergine (B), #1018 cornflower (C) and #1016 kiwi (D)
- Size M/N/13/9mm crochet hook or size needed to obtain gauge
- Size I/9/5.5mm crochet hook
- Tapestry needle

GAUGE
Size M/N hook and 2 strands of yarn held tog:
9 sc and 10 rows = 4 inches

PATTERN NOTES
Weave in ends as work progresses.

Join with slip stitch as indicated unless otherwise stated.

Chain-2 at beginning of row does not count as first half double crochet unless otherwise stated.

WING
Make 2.

Row 1: With M/N hook and 2 strands of A held tog, ch 4, sc in 2nd ch from hook and in next ch, 2 sc in last ch, turn. *(4 sc)*

Row 2: Ch 6, sc in 2nd ch from hook and in each of next 4 chs, sc in each sc across, turn. *(9 sc)*

Row 3: Ch 1, sc in each st across to last st, 2 sc in last st, turn. *(10 sc)*

Row 4: Ch 5, sc in 2nd ch from hook and in each of next 3 chs, sc in each sc across, turn. *(14 sc)*

Row 5: Rep row 3. *(15 sc)*

Row 6: Ch 3, sc in 2nd ch from hook and in next ch, sc in each sc across, turn. *(17 sc)*

Row 7: Rep row 3. *(18 sc)*

Row 8: Ch 1, 2 sc in first st, sc in each rem st across, turn. (19 sc)

Row 9: Ch 1, sc in each st across to last st, 2 sc in last st, turn. *(20 sc)*

Row 10: Rep row 8. *(21 sc)*

Row 11: Ch 1, **sc dec** *(see Stitch Guide)* in first 2 sts, sc in each st across to last st, 2 sc in last st, turn. *(21 sc)*

Rows 12 & 13: Rep rows 8 and 9. *(23 sts at end of last row)*

Row 14: Ch 1, sc in each st across, turn.

Row 15: Ch 1, sc in each st across to last st, 2 sc in last st, turn. *(24 sc)*

Row 16: Ch 1, sc in each st across to last 2 sts, sc dec in last 2 sts, turn. *(23 sc)*

Row 17: Ch 1, sc in each st across, turn.

Row 18: Ch 1, 2 sc in first st, sc in each st across to last 2 sts, sc dec in last 2 sts, turn. *(23 sc)*

Row 19: Rep row 15. *(24 sc)*

Row 20: Ch 4, sc in 2nd ch from hook and in each of next 2 chs, sc in each sc across, turn. *(27 sc)*

Row 21: Ch 1, sc dec in first 2 sts, sc in each rem st across, turn. *(26 sc)*

Row 22: Ch 1, sc in each st across to last 2 sts, sc dec in last 2 sts, turn. *(25 sc)*

Row 23: Ch 1, sc in each st across, turn.

Rows 24–27: [Rep rows 22 and 23 alternately] twice. *(23 sc at end of last row)*

Row 28: Rep row 22. *(22 sc)*

Rows 29 & 30: Rep rows 21 and 22. *(20 sc at end of last row)*

Row 31: Ch 2, sc in 2nd ch from hook and in each st across, turn. *(21 sc)*

Row 32: Ch 1, sc in each st across to last st, 2 sc in last st, turn. *(22 sc)*

Row 33: Ch 1, 2 sc in first st, sc in each rem st across, turn. *(23 sc)*

Rows 34 & 35: Rep rows 32 and 33. *(25 sc at end of last row)*

Row 36: Ch 1, sc in each st across, turn.

Row 37: Ch 1, 2 sc in first st, sc in each rem st across, turn. *(26 sc)*

Rows 38 & 39: Rep rows 36 and 37. *(27 sc at end of last row)*

Row 40: Rep row 36.

Row 41: Ch 1, 2 sc in first st, sc in each st across to last 4 sts, sc dec in next 2 sts, leaving rem sts unworked, turn. *(25 sc)*

Row 42: Ch 1, sc dec in first 2 sts, sc in each rem st across, turn. *(24 sc)*

Row 43: Ch 1, sc in each st across to last 2 sts, sc dec in last 2 sts. *(23 sc)*

Row 44: Ch 1, sc in each st across to last st, 2 sc in last st. *(24 sc)*

Row 45: Rep row 43. *(23 sc)*

Row 46: Ch 1, sc in each st across, turn.

Row 47: Rep row 43. *(22 sc)*

Row 48: Rep row 42. *(21 sc)*

Row 49: Ch 1, sc in each st across, turn.

Row 50: Ch 1, sc dec in first 2 sts, sc in each rem st across, turn. *(20 sc)*

Row 51: Ch 1, 2 sc in first st, sc in each st across to last 2 sts, sc dec in last 2 sts, turn. *(20 sc)*

Row 52: Rep row 50. *(19 sc)*

Row 53: Ch 1, sc in each st across to last 2 sts, sc dec in last 2 sts, turn. *(18 sc)*

Row 54: Ch 1, sc dec in first 2 sts, sc dec in next 2 sts, sc in each rem st across. *(16 sc)*

Row 55: Rep row 53. *(15 sc)*

Row 56: Ch 1, sc in each st across, turn.

Row 57: Ch 1, sc in each st across to last 3 sts, sc dec in next 2 sts, leaving last st unworked, turn. *(13 sc)*

Row 58: Ch 1, sc dec in first 2 sts, sc in each rem st across, turn. *(12 sc)*

Row 59: Ch 1, sc in each st across to last 4 sts, sc dec in next 2 sts, leaving rem sts unworked, turn. *(9 sc)*

Row 60: Ch 1, sc dec in first 2 sts, sc in each rem st across, turn. *(8 sc)*

Row 61: Ch 1, sc in each of first 3 sc, sc dec in next 2 sc, leaving rem sts unworked, turn. *(4 sc)*

Row 62: Ch 1, sc dec in first 2 sts, sc in each of last 2 sc. Fasten off.

Place straight edges of Wings tog and join by working sc through both thicknesses. Unfold wings. Seam is now on WS of piece.

EDGING

Rnd 1 (RS): With RS facing and with M/N hook and 2 strands of C held tog, **join** *(see Pattern Notes)* at either end of center seam, ch 1, sc evenly sp to outer corner, (sc, ch 1, sc) in corner st, sc evenly sp to 3 inner corner sts, sc dec in 3 inner corner sts, [sc evenly sp to outer corner, (sc, ch 1, sc) in corner st] twice, sc evenly sp to next 3 inner corner sts, sc dec in 3 inner corner sts, sc evenly sp to next outer corner, (sc, ch 1, sc) in corner st, sc evenly sp to first sc, join in first sc, turn.

Rnd 2: Ch 1, sc in each st to outer corner, (sc, ch 1, sc) in corner st, sc in each st to next 3 inner corner sts, sc dec in 3 inner corner sts, [sc in each st to next outer corner, (sc, ch 1, sc) in corner st] twice, sc in each sc to next 3 inner corner sts, sc dec in 3 inner corner sts, sc in each sc to next outer corner, (sc, ch 1, sc) in corner st, sc in each sc to first sc, join in first sc, turn.

Rnd 3: Rep rnd 2, **change color** *(see Stitch Guide)* to 2 strands of B held tog, turn. Fasten off C.

Rnd 4: Rep rnd 2. Fasten off.

BODY

Row 1 (RS): With I hook and B, ch 6, hdc in 3rd ch from hook and in each rem ch across, turn. *(4 hdc)*

Rows 2–5: **Ch 2** (*see Pattern Notes*), 2 hdc in first st, hdc in each st across to last st, 2 hdc in last st, turn. (*12 hdc*)

Rows 6–29: Ch 2, hdc in each st across, turn.

Row 30: Ch 2, **hdc dec** (*see Stitch Guide*) in first 2 sts, hdc in each st across to last 2 sts, hdc dec in last 2 sts, turn. (*10 hdc*)

Row 31: Ch 2, hdc dec in first 2 sts, hdc dec in next 2 sts, hdc in each of next 2 sts, [hdc dec in next 2 sts] twice, turn. (*6 hdc*)

EDGING
Work sc evenly sp around entire piece, join in first sc. Fasten off.

ANTENNAE
Make 2.

With I hook and B, ch 15, 3 sc in 2nd ch from hook and in each of next 4 chs, sc in each rem ch across. Leaving long end for sewing, fasten off. (*24 sc*)

DIAMOND
Make 2.

With I hook and D, ch 11, sl st in 2nd ch from hook, sc in next ch, hdc in next ch, dc in next ch, tr in each of next 2 chs, dc in next ch, hdc in next ch, sc in next ch, sl st in next ch, working in unused lps on opposite side of foundation ch, ch 1, sl st in first ch, sc in next ch, hdc in next ch, dc in next ch, tr in each of next 2 chs, dc in next ch, sc in next ch, sl st in next ch. Leaving long end for sewing, fasten off.

FLOWER PETAL
Make 2.

With I hook and B, ch 6, join in first ch to form ring, *ch 5, sc in 2nd ch from hook, dc in each of next 3 chs, sc in ring, rep from * 4 times. Leaving long end for sewing, fasten off.

FLOWER CENTER
Make 2.

With I hook and C, ch 4, join in first ch to form ring, ch 1, 6 sc in ring, join in first sc. Leaving long end for sewing, fasten off. (*6 sc*)

SMALL SPOT
Make 4 with D & 2 with C.

With I hook, ch 4, join in first ch to form ring. Leaving long end for sewing, fasten off.

LARGE SPOT
Make 2.

With I hook and B, ch 4, join in first ch to form ring, ch 1, 7 sc in ring, join in first sc. Leaving long end for sewing, fasten off. (*7 sc*)

FINISHING
Referring to photo for placement, sew Body to Wings. Sew bases of antennae behind edge of Body. Sew Centers to Petals with WS facing. Sew Flowers, Diamonds and Spots to Body. ∎

Granny Shell
TURTLE

SKILL LEVEL

EASY

FINISHED MEASUREMENTS
24 inches wide x 46 inches from head to tail

MATERIALS
- Deborah Norville Everyday Soft Worsted Solids medium (worsted) weight acrylic yarn (4 oz/203 yds/113g per skein):
    3 skeins #1015 sagebrush (A)
    1 skein each #1016 kiwi (B),
      #1028 mustard (C),
      #1001 snow white (D) and
      #1011 chocolate
- Size M/N/13/9mm crochet hook or size needed to obtain gauge
- Size I/9/5.5mm crochet hook
- Tapestry needle
- Stitch marker

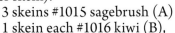

GAUGE
Size M/N hook and 2 strands of yarn held tog:
  9 sc and 10 rows = 4 inches

PATTERN NOTES
Weave in ends as work progresses.

Join with slip stitch as indicated unless otherwise stated.

Chain-2 at beginning of round counts as first double crochet unless otherwise stated.

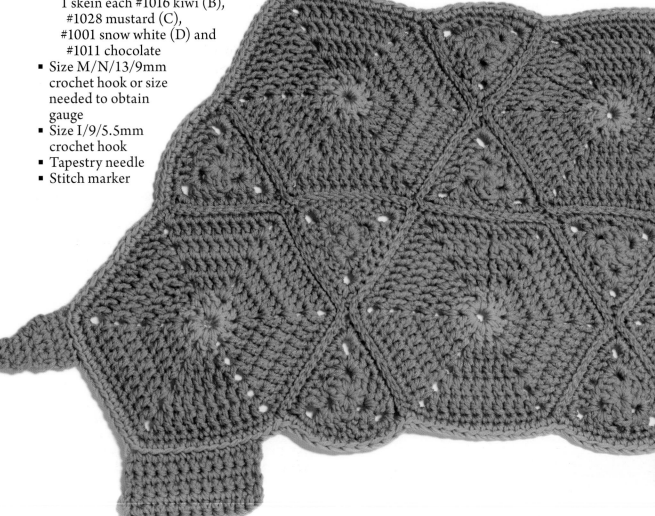

SHELL

HEXAGONS
Make 5.

Rnd 1 (RS): With M/N hook and 2 strands of C held tog, ch 6, **join** (see Pattern Notes) in first ch to form ring, **ch 2** (see Pattern Notes), dc in ring, ch 1, [2 dc in ring, ch 1] 5 times, join in 2nd ch of beg ch-2, **changing color** (see Stitch Guide) to 2 strands of A held tog. Fasten off C. (12 dc)

Rnd 2: Ch 2, dc in next st, (dc, ch 2, dc) in next ch-1 sp, *dc in each of next 2 sts, (dc, ch 2, dc) in next ch-1 sp, rep from * 4 times, join in first st. (24 dc)

Rnd 3: Ch 2, dc in each of next 2 sts, (dc, ch 2, dc) in next ch-2 sp, *dc in each of next 4 sts, (dc, ch 2, dc) in next ch-2 sp, rep from * 4 times, dc in next st, join in first st, changing color to 2 strands of B held tog. Do not fasten off A. (36 dc)

Rnd 4: Ch 2, dc in each of next 3 sts, (dc, ch 2, dc) in next ch-2 sp, *dc in each of next 6 sts, (dc, ch 2, dc) in next ch-2 sp, rep from * 4 more times, dc in each of next 2 sts, join in first st using 2 strands of A held tog, carried up from row 2. Fasten off B. (48 dc)

Rnd 5: Ch 2, dc in each of next 4 sts, (dc, ch 2, dc) in next ch-2 sp, * dc in each of next 8 sts, (dc, ch 2, dc) in next ch-2 sp, rep from * 4 more times, dc in each of next 3 sts, join in first st.

Rnd 6: Ch 1, sc in same st as beg ch-1, sc in each of next 5 sts, (sc, ch 1, sc) in next ch-2 sp, *sc in each of next 10 sts, (sc, ch 1, sc) in next ch-2 sp, rep from * 4 times, sc in each of next 4 sts, join in first st. Fasten off.

TRIANGLE
Make 8.

Rnd 1 (RS): With M/N hook and 2 strands of B held tog, ch 4, join in first ch to form ring, ch 2, dc in ring, ch 1, [2 dc in ring, ch 1] twice, join in first st. Fasten off.

Rnd 2 (RS): With RS facing and with M/N hook and 2 strands of A held tog, join in any ch-1 sp, ch 2, (2 dc, ch 3, 3 dc) in same sp as join, (3 dc, ch 3, 3 dc) in each of next 2 ch-1 sps, join in first st.

Rnd 3: Ch 1, sc in same st as beg ch-1, sc in each of next 2 sts, (2 sc, ch 3, 2 sc) in next ch-3 sp, *sc in each of next 6 sts, (2 sc, ch 3, 2 sc) in next ch-3 sp, rep from * once, sc in each of next 3 sts, join in first st. Fasten off.

ASSEMBLE
Referring to diagram for placement and with M/N hook and A, sl st pieces tog.

EDGING
With M/N hook and 2 strands of C held tog, join anywhere along edge of Shell, ch 1, sc evenly sp around Shell, working 2 sc in each corner ch-1 sp, join in first st. Fasten off.

LEG
Make 2.

Note: Mark rightmost 12 sts and leftmost 12 sts of straight bottom edge of Shell for placement of Legs.

Row 1 (RS): Hold shell upside down and with RS facing, with M/N hook and 2 strands of B held tog, join in **back lp** (see Stitch Guide) of first marked st, working in back lps, ch 1, sc in same st as beg ch-1, sc in each of next 11 sts, turn. (12 sc)

Rows 2–6: Ch 1, sc in each st across. At end of last row, fasten off. Remove markers.

HEAD
Row 1 (RS): With RS facing, and with M/N hook and 2 strands of B held tog, join in back lp of next unworked st from right Leg, ch 1, working in back lps, sc in same st as beg ch-1, sc in each of next 13 sts, turn. (14 sc)

Row 2: Ch 1, 2 sc in first st, sc in each st across to last 2 sts, **sc dec** *(see Stitch Guide)* in last 2 sts, turn. *(14 sc)*

Row 3: Ch 1, sc in each st across, turn.

Row 4: Ch 1, sc in each st across to last 2 sts, sc dec in last 2 sts, turn. *(13 sc)*

Row 5: Ch 1, sc dec in first 2 sts, sc in each rem st across, turn. *(12 sc)*

Row 6: Rep row 2. *(12 sc)*

Row 7: Ch 1, sc dec in first 2 sts, sc in each st across to last st, 2 sc in last st, turn. *(12 sc)*

Row 8: Ch 1, 2 sc in first st, sc in each rem st across, turn. *(13 sc)*

Row 9: Ch 1, sc in each st across, turn.

Rows 10 & 11: Rep rows 8 and 9. *(14 sts)*

Row 12: Ch 1, sc in each st across, turn.

Row 13: Ch 1, sc in each st across to last st, 2 sc in last st, turn. *(15 sc)*

Rows 14 & 15: Ch 1, sc in each st across, turn.

Row 16: Ch 1, sc dec in first 2 sts, sc in each st across to last 2 sts, sc dec in last 2 sts, turn. *(13 sc)*

Row 17: Ch 1, sc in each st across, turn.

Row 18: Rep row 16. *(11 sc)*

Row 19: Ch 1, sc dec in first 2 sts, sc dec in next 2 sts, sc in each st across to last 2 sts, sc dec in last 2 sts. *(8 sc)*

Row 20: Ch 1, sc dec in first 2 sts, sc in each of next 2 sc, [sc dec in next 2 sts] twice. Fasten off. *(5 sc)*

TAIL
Note: *Count back 13 unworked sts from left Leg and mark next st for Tail placement.*

Row 1 (RS): With RS facing, and with M/N hook and 2 strands of B held tog, join in back lp of marked st, working in back lps, ch 1, sc in same st as beg ch-1, sc in each of next 4 sts, turn. *(5 sc)*

Rows 2 & 3: Ch 1, sc in each st across, turn.

Row 4: Ch 1, sc dec in first 2 sts, sc in next sc, sc dec in last 2 sts, turn. *(3 sc)*

Rows 5 & 6: Rep rows 2 and 3.

Row 7: Ch 1, sc dec in first 2 sts, sc in last st, turn. *(2 sc)*

Row 8: Ch 1, sc in each st across, turn.

Row 9: Ch 1, sc dec in first 2 sts. Fasten off. *(1 sc)*

EYE
EYEBALL
Rnd 1 (RS): With I hook and D, ch 4, join in first ch to form ring, ch 1, 7 sc in ring, join in first sc. *(7 sc)*

Rnd 2: Ch 1, 2 sc in each st around, join in first sc. Leaving long end for sewing, fasten off. *(14 sc)*

PUPIL
With I hook and E, ch 4, join in first ch to form ring, ch 1, 7 sc in ring, join in first sc. Leaving long end for sewing, fasten off. *(7 sc)*

FINISHING
Sew Pupil to center of Eyeball. Referring to photo for placement, sew Eye to Head. ∎

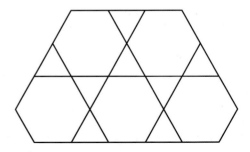

Granny Shell Turtle Rug
Assembly Diagram

Baby ELEPHANT

SKILL LEVEL

EASY

FINISHED MEASUREMENTS
36 inches wide x 24 inches long

MATERIALS
- Deborah Norville Everyday Soft Worsted Solids medium (worsted) weight acrylic yarn (4 oz/203 yds/113g per skein):
  - 3 skeins #1024 steel (A)
  - 1 skein each #1006 baby pink (B), #1001 snow white (C) and #1012 black (D)
- Size M/N/13/9mm crochet hook or size needed to obtain gauge
- Size I/9/5.5mm crochet hook
- Tapestry needle
- Stitch markers

GAUGE
Size M/N hook and 2 strands of yarn held tog: 9 sc and 10 rows = 4 inches

PATTERN NOTES
Weave in ends as work progresses.

Join with slip stitch as indicated unless otherwise stated.

BODY & HEAD
Row 1 (RS): With M/N hook and 2 strands of A held tog, ch 15, sc in 2nd ch from hook and in each rem ch across, turn. *(14 sc)*

Row 2: Ch 1, 2 sc in first st, 2 sc in next st, sc in each st across to last 2 sts, 2 sc in each of last 2 sts, turn. *(18 sc)*

Row 3: Ch 1, 2 sc in first st, sc in each st across to last st, 2 sc in last st, turn. *(20 sc)*

Row 4: Rep row 2. *(24 sc)*

Rows 5–12: Rep row 3. *(40 sc at end of last row)*

Row 13: Ch 1, sc in each st across, turn.

Row 14: Ch 1, 2 sc in first st, sc in each st across to last st, 2 sc in last st, turn. *(42 sc)*

Rows 15–18: [Rep rows 13 and 14 alternately] twice. *(46 sc)*

Row 19: Rep row 13.

Row 20: Ch 7, sc in 2nd ch from hook and each of next 5 chs, sc in each rem st across, turn. *(52 sc)*

Row 21: Rep row 14. *(54 sc)*

Row 22: Ch 8 *(mark last ch for Trunk placement)*, sc in 2nd ch from hook and in each of next 6 chs, sc in each rem st across, turn. *(61 sc)*

Row 23: Ch 1, sc in each st across to last 2 sts, 2 sc in each of last 2 sts, turn. *(63 sc)*

Row 24: Ch 1, 2 sc in first st, 2 sc in next st, sc in each st across to last st, 2 sc in last st, turn. *(66 sc)*

Row 25: Ch 1, sc in each st across to last st, 2 sc in last st, turn. *(67 sc)*

Row 26: Ch 1, sc in each st across, turn.

Row 27: Ch 1, sc in each st across to last st, 2 sc in last st, turn. *(68 sc)*

Rows 28–40: Ch 1, sc in each st across, turn.

Row 41: Ch 1, sc in each st across to last 2 sts, **sc dec** *(see Stitch Guide)* in last 2 sts, turn. *(67 sc)*

Rows 42 & 43: Ch 1, sc in each st across, turn.

Rows 44–46: Ch 1, sc dec in first 2 sts, sc in each rem st across, turn. *(64 sc)*

Row 47: Ch 1, sc in each st across, turn.

Row 48: Ch 1, sc dec in first 2 sts, sc in each st across to last 2 sts, sc dec in last 2 sts, turn. *(62 sc)*

Rows 49 & 50: Ch 1, sc dec in first 2 sts, sc in each rem st across, turn. *(60 sc)*

Row 51: Ch 1, sc dec in first 2 sts, sc in each of next 44 sts, mark next st for Head placement, leaving marked st and rem sts unworked, turn. *(45 sc)*

Rows 52–54: Rep row 48. *(39 sc at end of last row)*

Row 55: Ch 1, sc dec in first 2 sts, sc dec in next 2 sts, sc in each st across to last 4 sts, [sc dec in next 2 sts] twice, turn. *(35 sc)*

Row 56: Rep row 48. *(33 sc)*

Row 57: Rep row 55. *(29 sc)*

Row 58: Ch 1, sc dec in first 2 sts, [sc dec in next 2 sts] twice, sc in each st across to last 6 sts, [sc dec in next 2 sts] 3 times, turn. *(23 sc)*

Row 59: Ch 1, sc in each of first 3 sts, [sc dec in next 2 sts] twice, sc in each st across to last 7 sts, [sc dec in next 2 sts] twice, sc in each of last 3 sts. Fasten off. *(19 sc)*

TOP OF HEAD

Row 1 (RS): With RS facing and with M/N hook and 2 strands of A held tog, **join** *(see Pattern Notes)* in marked st on Row 51, ch 1, sc in same st as beg ch-1, sc in each st across to last 2 sts, sc dec in last 2 sts, turn. *(13 sc)*

Rows 2 & 3: Ch 1, sc dec in first 2 sts, sc dec in next 2 sts, sc in each st across to last 4 sts, [sc dec in next 2 sts] twice, turn. At end of row 3, fasten off. Remove Head marker. *(5 sc)*

FOOT
Make 2.

Note: *Mark each edge st of rows 6 and 15 of Body. Foot is worked on either side of Body from marked st to marked st.*

Row 1 (WS): With WS facing and with M/N hook and 2 strands of A held tog, join in first marked st on 1 side of Body, ch 1, sc in same st as beg ch-1, sc in each of next 9 edge sts, ending in 2nd marked st, turn. *(10 sc)*

Rows 2–7: Ch 1, sc in each sc across, turn. At end of last row, fasten off. Remove markers.

Work 2nd Leg in same manner on other side of Body.

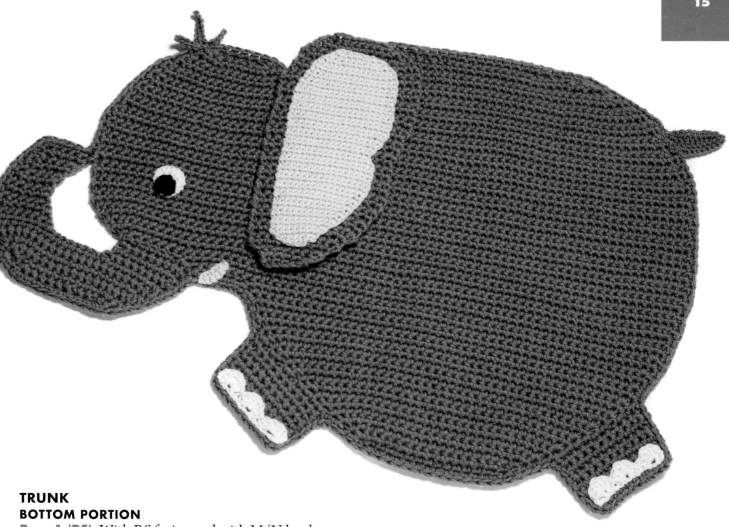

TRUNK

BOTTOM PORTION

Row 1 (RS): With RS facing and with M/N hook and 2 strands of A held tog, join in marked ch on row 22 of Head, ch 1, sc in same ch as beg ch-1, working in unused lps on opposite side of ch-8, sc in each of next 7 chs, sc in side of next row on Head, turn. *(9 sc)*

Rows 2 & 3: Ch 1, sc in each st across, turn.

Row 4: Ch 1, sc dec in first 2 sts, sc in each st across to last st, 2 sc in last st, turn. *(9 sc)*

Row 5: Ch 16, sc in 2nd ch from hook and in each of next 14 chs, sc in each st across to last 2 sts, sc dec in last 2 sts, turn. *(23 sc)*

Row 6: Ch 1, sc in each st across to last 2 sts, sc dec in last 2 sts, turn. *(22 sc)*

Row 7: Ch 1, sc dec in first 2 sts, sc dec in next 2 sts, sc in each st across to last 2 sts, sc dec in last 2 sts, turn. *(19 sc)*

Row 8: Ch 1, sc dec in first 2 sts, sc in each st across to last 4 sts, [sc dec in next 2 sts] twice, turn. *(16 sc)*

Row 9: Rep row 7. *(13 sc)*

Row 10: Ch 1, sc in first st, [sc dec in next 2 sts, sc in next st] twice, sc in each st across to last 2 sts, sc dec in last 2 sts. Fasten off. Remove Trunk marker. *(10 sc)*

TOP PORTION

Row 1 (WS): Hold Bottom Portion with WS facing and unused lps of ch-16 of row 5 at top, with M/N hook and 2 strands of A held tog, join in first ch at right-hand edge, ch 1, working in unused lps on opposite side of ch-16, sc in same ch as beg ch-1, sc in each of next 5 chs, sc dec in next 2 chs, leaving rem chs unworked, turn. *(7 sc)*

Row 2: Ch 1, sc in each st across, turn.

Row 3: Ch 1, sc dec in first 2 sts, sc in each st across to last 2 sts, sc dec in last 2 sts, turn. *(5 sc)*

Rows 4–6: Rep row 2.

Row 7: Ch 1, sc dec in first 2 sts, sc in each st across to last st, 2 sc in last st, turn. (*5 sc*)

Row 8: Rep row 2.

Row 9: Rep row 7.

Row 10: Ch 1, 2 sc in first st, sc in each st across to last 2 sts, sc dec in last 2 sts, turn. (*5 sc*)

Row 11: Ch 1, sc in each st across, join in edge st of row 33 of Body, turn.

EDGING
With RS facing, ch 1, work sc evenly sp around entire piece, working 3 sc in each Foot corner, join in first sc. Fasten off.

EAR
OUTER SECTION
Row 1 (RS): With M/N hook and 2 strands of A held tog, ch 6, sc in 2nd ch from hook and in each rem ch across, turn. (*5 sc*)

Rows 2 & 3: Ch 1, 2 sc in first st, sc in each st across to last st, 2 sc in last st, turn. (*9 sc at end of last row*)

Row 4: Ch 1, sc in each st across to last st, 2 sc in last st, turn. (*10 sc*)

Row 5: Ch 1, 2 sc in first st, sc in each rem st across, turn. (*11 sc*)

Row 6: Rep row 4. (*12 sc*)

Rows 7 & 8: Ch 1, sc in each st across, turn.

Row 9: Rep row 5. (*13 sc*)

Row 10: Rep row 7.

Row 11: Rep row 5. (*14 sc*)

Rows 12–18: Rep row 7.

Row 19: Rep row 5. (*15 sc*)

Rows 20 & 21: Rep row 7.

Row 22: Ch 1, sc in each st across to last st, 2 sc in last st, turn. (*16 sc*)

Rows 23–28: Rep row 7.

Row 29: Ch 1, sc dec in first 2 sts, sc in each rem st across, turn. (*15 sc*)

Rows 30 & 31: Rep row 7.

Rows 32–34: Ch 1, sc dec in first 2 sts, sc in each st across to last 2 sts, sc dec in last 2 sts. (*9 sc at end of last row*)

Row 35: Ch 1, sc dec in first 2 sts, sc dec in next 2 sts, sc in each st across to last 2 sts, sc dec in last 2 sts. Fasten off. (*6 sc*)

INNER SECTION
Row 1 (WS): With I hook and B, ch 6, sc in 2nd ch from hook and in each rem ch across, turn. (*5 sc*)

Rows 2 & 3: Ch 1, 2 sc in first st, sc in each st across to last st, 2 sc in last st, turn. (*9 sc*)

Row 4: Ch 1, 2 sc in first st, sc in each rem st across, turn. (*10 sc*)

Row 5: Ch 1, sc in each st across to last st, 2 sc in last st, turn. (*11 sc*)

Row 6: Ch 1, 2 sc in first st, sc in each rem st across, turn. (*12 sc*)

Row 7: Ch 1, sc in each st across, turn.

Rows 8–15: [Rep rows 6 and 7 alternately] 4 times. (*16 sc at end of last row*)

Rows 16–20: Ch 1, sc in each st across, turn.

Row 21: Ch 1, sc in each st across to last 2 sts, sc dec in last 2 sts, turn. (*15 sc*)

Row 22: Ch 1, sc in each st across, turn.

Row 23: Ch 1, sc in each st across to last st, 2 sc in last st, turn. (*16 sc*)

Rows 24–27: [Rep rows 22 and 23 alternately] twice. (*18 sc at end last row*)

Rows 28–36: Rep row 22.

Row 37: Ch 1, sc dec in first 2 sts, sc in each rem st across, turn. *(17 sc)*

Row 38: Ch 1, sc in each st across, turn.

Rows 39 & 40: Rep rows 37 and 38. *(16 sc at end of last row)*

Row 41: Rep row 38.

Row 42: Ch 1, sc dec in first 2 sts, sc in each st across to last 2 sts, sc dec in last 2 sts, turn. *(14 sc)*

Row 43: Ch 1, sc dec in first 2 sts, sc dec in next 2 sts, sc in each st across to last 4 sts, [sc dec in next 2 sts] twice, turn. *(10 sc)*

Row 44: Rep row 42. Fasten off. *(8 sc)*

TOE
Make 2.

Row 1 (RS): With I hook and C, ch 18, (2 dc, tr, 2 dc) in 3rd ch from hook, *sk next 2 chs, sl st in next ch, sk next 2 chs, (2 dc, tr, 2 dc) in next ch, rep from * once, sk next 2 chs, sl st in last ch. Leaving long end for sewing, fasten off.

EYE
Make 2.

EYEBALL
Rnd 1 (RS): With I hook and C, ch 4, join in first ch to form ring, ch 1, 7 sc in ring, join in first sc. *(7 sc)*

Rnd 2: Ch 1, 2 sc in each st around, join in first sc. Leaving long end for sewing, fasten off. *(14 sc)*

PUPIL
With I hook and D, ch 4, join in first ch to form ring, ch 1, 7 sc in ring, join in first sc. Fasten off. *(7 sc)*

MOUTH
With I hook and B, ch 7, sl st in 2nd ch from hook, sc in each of next 5 chs. Leaving long end for sewing, fasten off.

TUFT
Row 1 (RS): With I hook and A, ch 6, sl st in 2nd ch from hook and in each rem ch, do not turn.

Row 2: Ch 8, sl st in 2nd ch from hook, sc in each of next 6 chs, do not turn.

Row 3: Ch 6, sl st in 2nd ch from hook and in each of next 4 chs, join in first foundation ch of row 1. Leaving long end for sewing, fasten off.

TAIL
Row 1 (RS): With I hook and A, ch 11, sl st in 2nd ch from hook, sc in next ch, hdc in each of next 2 chs, dc in each of next 4 chs, tr in each of last 2 chs, turn.

Row 2: Ch 1, sc in each st across, sc in end of row 1, working in unused lps on opposite side of foundation ch, sc in each ch across. Leaving long end for sewing, fasten off.

FINISHING
Place Inner Section of Ear at center of Outer Section. With B, sew pieces together. Do not work all way through Gray Section when sewing so B does not show on opposite side.

Referring to photo for placement, sew Ear along left side edge only. With RS of Pupils facing WS of Eyeballs, sew pieces together. With WS of Eyeballs facing, sew Eyeballs to Head. With WS facing, sew Mouth to Head. With RS facing, sew Toes, Tuft and Tail to Body. ■

Mischievous
MONKEY

SKILL LEVEL

EASY

FINISHED MEASUREMENTS
27 inches wide x 25 inches long

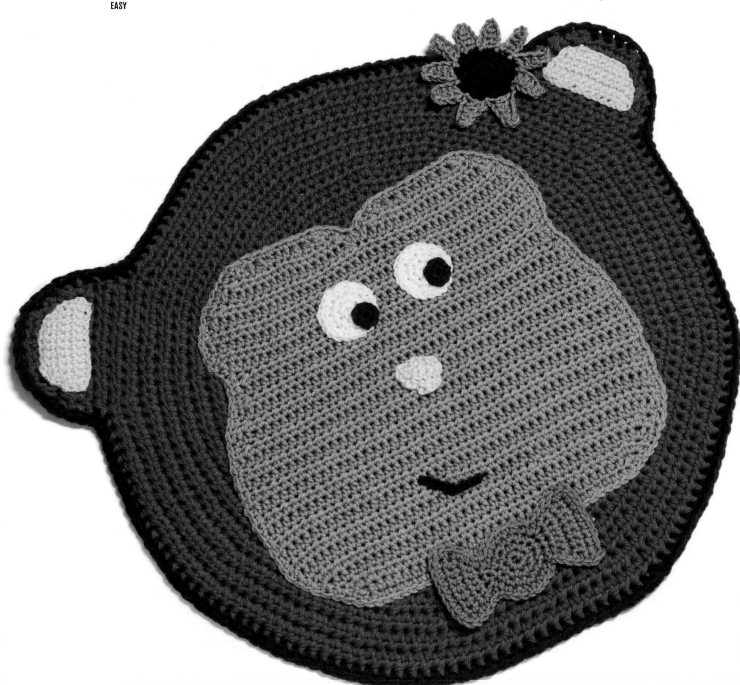

MATERIALS

- Deborah Norville Everyday Soft Worsted Solids medium (worsted) weight acrylic yarn (4 oz/203 yds/ 113g per skein):
    - 3 skeins #1034 terra cotta (A)
    - 1 skein each #1014 caramel (B), #1011 chocolate (C), #1006 baby pink (D), #1018 cornflower (E), #1001 snow white (F), #1020 orchid (G) and #1010 aubergine (H)
- Size M/N/13/9mm crochet hook or size needed to obtain gauge
- Size I/9/5.5mm crochet hook
- Tapestry needle
- Stitch markers

GAUGE

Size M/N hook and 2 strands of yarn held tog: 9 sc and 10 rows = 4 inches

PATTERN NOTES

Weave in ends as work progresses.

Join with slip stitch as indicated unless otherwise stated.

Chain-2 at beginning of row or round does not count as half double crochet unless otherwise stated.

HEAD

Note: *Head is worked on WS in continuous rnds. Do not join unless specified; mark beg of rnds.*

Rnd 1 (WS): With M/N hook and 2 strands of A held tog, ch 5, **join** *(see Pattern Notes)* in first ch to form ring, **ch 2** *(see Pattern Notes)*, 8 hdc in ring. *(8 hdc)*

Rnd 2: 2 hdc in each st around. *(16 hdc)*

Rnd 3: *Hdc in next st, 2 hdc in next st, rep from * around. *(24 sts)*

Rnd 4: *Hdc in each of next 2 sts, 2 hdc in next st, rep from * around. *(32 sts)*

Rnds 5–18: Rep rnd 4, having 1 additional st between inc on each rem rnd. *(144 hdc)*

EARS

FIRST EAR

Row 1 (WS): Hdc in each of next 11 sts, leaving rem sts unworked, turn. *(11 hdc)*

Row 2: Ch 2, hdc in each st across turn.

Rows 3–5: Ch 2, **hdc dec** *(see Stitch Guide)* in first 2 sts, hdc in each st across to last 2 sts, hdc dec in last 2 sts, turn. At end of last row, fasten off. *(5 hdc at end of last row)*

2ND EAR

Row 1 (WS): With WS facing, sk next 43 unworked sts from First Ear, with M/N hook and 2 strands of A held tog, join in next st, ch 2, hdc in same st as beg ch-2, hdc in each of next 10 sts, leaving rem sts unworked, turn. *(11 hdc)*

Rows 2–5: Rep rows 2–5 of First Ear.

EDGING

With RS facing and with M/N hook and 2 strands of C held tog, join anywhere along edge, ch 1, sc in same sp as beg ch-1, sc evenly sp around, join in first sc. Fasten off.

FACE

Row 1 (RS): With I hook and B, ch 35, hdc in 3rd ch from hook and in each rem ch across, turn. *(33 hdc)*

Row 2: Ch 2, 2 hdc in first st, 2 hdc in next st, hdc in each st across to last 2 sts, 2 hdc in each of last 2 sts, turn. *(37 hdc)*

Row 3: Ch 2, 2 hdc in first st, hdc in each st across to last st, 2 hdc in last st, turn. *(39 hdc)*

Rows 4 & 5: Rep rows 2 and 3. *(45 hdc at end of last row)*

Rows 6–15: Ch 2, hdc in each st across, turn.

Row 16: Ch 2, hdc dec in first 2 sts, hdc in each st across to last 2 sts, hdc dec in last 2 sts, turn. *(43 hdc)*

Row 17: Ch 2, hdc in each st across, turn.

Rows 18–21: [Rep rows 16 and 17 alternately] twice. *(39 hdc at end of last row)*

Row 22: Rep row 16. *(37 hdc)*

Row 23: Ch 2, 3 hdc in first st, hdc in each st across to last st, 3 hdc in last st, turn. *(41 hdc)*

Rows 24–26: Ch 2, hdc in each st across, turn.

Rows 27 & 28: Ch 2, hdc dec in first 2 sts, hdc in each st across to last 2 sts, hdc dec in last 2 sts, turn. *(37 hdc at end of last row)*

Row 29: Ch 2, hdc dec in first 2 sts, hdc in each of next 15 sts, hdc dec in next 2 sts, leaving rem sts unworked, turn. *(17 hdc)*

Row 30: Ch 2, hdc dec in first 2 sts, hdc in each st across to last 2 sts, hdc dec in last 2 sts, turn. *(15 hdc)*

Row 31: Ch 2, hdc dec in first 2 sts, [hdc dec in next 2 sts] twice, hdc in each of next 3 hdc, [hdc dec in next 2 sts] 3 times. Fasten off. *(9 hdc)*

LEFT HALF OF FACE
Row 1 (RS): With I hook, join B in center st of row 28 of Face, ch 1, hdc dec in same st as beg ch-1 and next st, hdc in each of next 15 sts, hdc dec in last 2 sts, turn. *(17 hdc)*

Row 2: Ch 2, hdc dec in first 2 sts, hdc in each st across to last 2 sts, hdc dec in last 2 sts, turn. *(15 hdc)*

Row 3: Ch 2, hdc dec in first 2 sts, [hdc dec in next 2 sts] twice, hdc in each of next 3 hdc, [hdc dec in next 2 sts] 3 times. *(9 hdc)*

EDGING
Ch 1, work sc evenly sp around piece, join in first sc. Fasten off.

INNER EAR
Make 2.

Row 1 (RS): With I hook and D, ch 13, sc in 2nd ch from hook and in each rem ch across, turn. *(12 sc)*

Row 2: Ch 1, sc in each st across, turn.

Row 3: Ch 1, sc dec in first 2 sts, sc in each st across to last 2 sts, sc dec in last 2 sts, turn. *(10 sc)*

Rows 4 & 5: Rep rows 2 and 3. *(8 sc at end of last row)*

Row 6: Rep row 3. Leaving long end for sewing, fasten off. *(6 sc)*

NOSE
Row 1 (RS): With I hook and D, ch 6, sc in 2nd ch from hook and in each rem ch across, turn. *(5 sc)*

Row 2: Ch 1, sc in each of first 3 sts, sc dec in last 2 sts, turn. *(4 sc)*

Row 3: Ch 1, sc dec in first 2 sts, sc in each of last 2 sts, turn. *(3 sc)*

Row 4: Ch 1, sc dec in first 2 sts, sc in last st. Leaving long end for sewing, fasten off.

EYE
Make 2.

EYEBALL
Rnd 1 (RS): With I hook and F, ch 4, join in first ch to form ring, ch 1, 7 sc in ring, join in first sc. *(7 sc)*

Rnd 2: Ch 1, 2 sc in each st around, join in first sc. *(14 sc)*

Rnd 3: Ch 1, sc in same st as beg ch-1, 2 sc in next st, *sc in next st, 2 sc in next st, rep from * around, join in first sc. Leaving long end for sewing, fasten off. *(21 sc)*

PUPIL
With I hook and C, ch 4, join in first ch to form ring, ch 1, 7 sc in ring, join in first sc. Leaving long end for sewing, fasten off. *(7 sc)*

MOUTH
With I hook and C, ch 10. Leaving long end for sewing, fasten off.

FLOWER (OPTIONAL)
CENTER
With H, work same as Eyeball.

PETALS
Rnd 1 (RS): With I hook, join G in any st on Center, *ch 6, hdc in 3rd ch from hook and in

next ch, dc in each of next 2 chs, sk next st on Center, sl st in next st on Center; rep from * 9 times. Fasten off.

BOWTIE (OPTIONAL)
CENTER
Rnd 1 (RS): With I hook and E, ch 4, join in first ch to form ring, ch 1, 7 sc in ring, join in first sc. *(7 sc)*

Rnd 2: Ch 1, 2 sc in each st around, join in first sc. *(14 sc)*

Rnd 3: Ch 1, sc in same st as beg ch-1, 2 sc in next st, *sc in next st, 2 sc in next st, rep from * around, join in first sc. Leaving long end for sewing, fasten off. *(21 sc)*

LEFT HALF
Row 1 (RS): Ch 1, now working in rows, sc in each of first 3 sts, leaving rem sts unworked, turn. *(3 sc)*

Row 2: Ch 1, 2 sc in each st across, turn. *(6 sc)*

Row 3: Ch 1, 2 sc in first st, sc in each st across to last st, 2 sc in last st. *(8 sc)*

Rows 4 & 5: Ch 1, sc in each st across, turn. At end of last row, fasten off.

RIGHT HALF
Row 1 (RS): With RS facing and I hook, sk next 8 unworked sts on Center, join E in next st, ch 1, sc in same st as beg ch-1, sc in each of next 2 sts, turn. *(3 sc)*

Rows 2–5: Rep rows 2–5 of Left Half. At end of last row, do not fasten off.

EDGING
Ch 1, sc evenly sp around edge, working 3 sc in each corner st, join in first sc. Fasten off.

FINISHING
Sew Pupils to center of Eyeballs. Referring to photo for placement, sew Eyes, Nose and Mouth and optional Flower or Bowtie to Face. ■

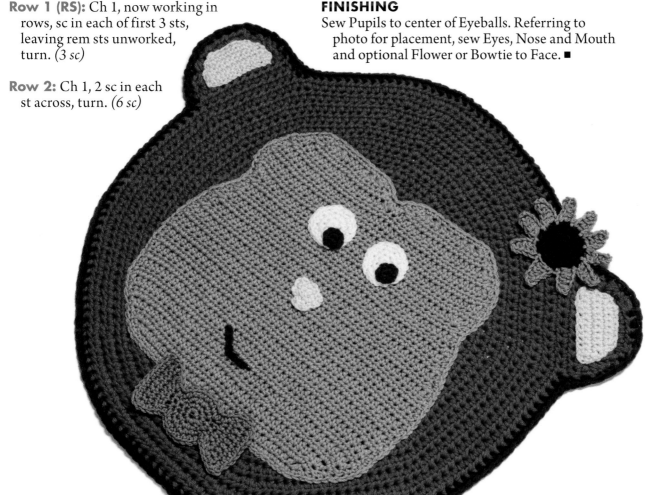

Sammy THE STEGOSAURUS

SKILL LEVEL

EASY

FINISHED MEASUREMENTS

25 inches wide x 37 inches long

MATERIALS

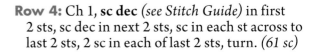

- Deborah Norville Everyday Soft Worsted Solids medium (worsted) weight acrylic yarn (4 oz/203 yds/ 113g per skein):

  3 skeins #1038 electric green (A)

  1 skein each #1022 bittersweet (B), #1028 mustard (C), #1001 snow white (D) and #1012 black (E)
- Size M/N/13/9mm crochet hook or size needed to obtain gauge
- Size I/9/5.5mm crochet hook
- Tapestry needle
- Stitch markers

GAUGE

Size M/N hook and 2 strands of yarn held tog:
9 sc and 10 rows = 4 inches

PATTERN NOTES

Weave in ends as work progresses.

Join with slip stitch as indicated unless otherwise stated.

BODY

Row 1 (WS): With M/N hook and 2 strands of A held tog, ch 58, sc in 2nd ch from hook and in each rem ch across, turn. *(57 sc)*

Rows 2 & 3: Ch 1, 2 sc in first st, sc in each st across to last st, 2 sc in last st, turn. *(61 sc at end of last row)*

Row 4: Ch 1, **sc dec** *(see Stitch Guide)* in first 2 sts, sc dec in next 2 sts, sc in each st across to last 2 sts, 2 sc in each of last 2 sts, turn. *(61 sc)*

Row 5: Ch 1, 2 sc in each of first 2 sts, sc in each st across to last 4 sts, [sc dec in next 2 sts] twice, turn. *(61 sc)*

Row 6: Ch 1, sc dec in first 2 sts, sc in each st across to last st, 2 sc in last st, turn.

Row 7: Ch 3, sc in 2nd ch from hook and in next ch, sc in each sc across to last 4 sts, sc dec in next 2 sts, leaving last 2 sts unworked, turn. *(60 sc)*

Row 8: Rep row 6.

Row 9: Ch 4, sc in 2nd ch from hook and in each of next 2 chs, sc in each st across to last 2 sts, sc dec in last 2 sts, turn. *(62 sc)*

Row 10: Rep row 6.

Row 11: Ch 5, sc in 2nd ch from hook and in each of next 3 chs, sc in each st across to last 2 sts, sc dec in last 2 sts, turn. *(65 sc)*

Row 12: Ch 1, sc in each of first 47 sts, sc dec in next 2 sts, sk next 2 sts, mark next st, leaving rem sts unworked, turn. *(48 sc)*

Row 13: Ch 1, sc dec in first 2 sts, sc in each st across to last 2 sts, sc dec in last 2 sts, turn. *(46 sc)*

Row 14: Ch 1, sc in each st across to last 2 sts, sc dec in last 2 sts, turn. *(45 sc)*

Rows 15 & 16: Rep rows 13 and 14. *(42 sc)*

Row 17: Rep row 13. *(40 sc)*

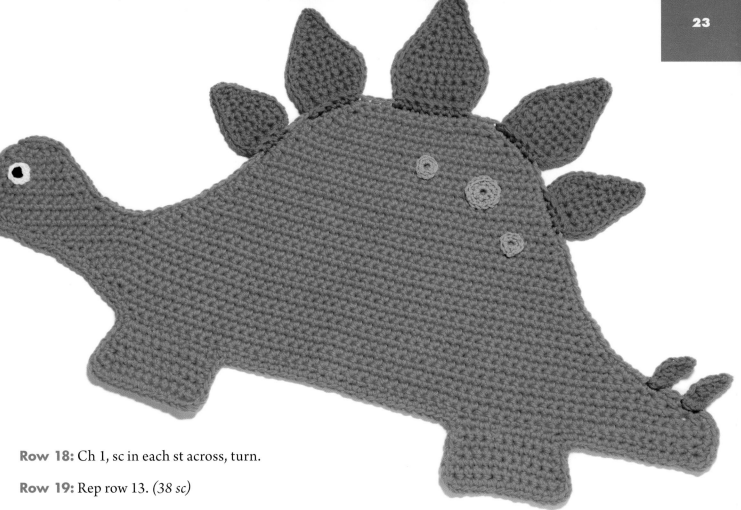

Row 18: Ch 1, sc in each st across, turn.

Row 19: Rep row 13. *(38 sc)*

Rows 20–29: Rep row 14. *(28 sc at end of last row)*

Rows 30–32: Rep row 13. *(22 sc at end of last row)*

Row 33: Ch 1, sc dec in first 2 sts, sc dec in next 2 sts, sc in each st across to last 4 sts, [sc dec in next 2 sts] twice, turn. *(18 sc)*

Row 34: Ch 1, sc dec in first 2 sts, sc in each of next 3 sts, sc dec in next 2 sts, sc in each of next 4 sts, sc dec in next 2 sts, sc in each of next 3 sts, sc dec in last 2 sts. Fasten off. *(14 sc)*

FIRST LEG
Row 1 (RS): Hold piece with RS facing and foundation ch at top, with M/N hook and 2 strands of A held tog, working in unused lps on opposite side of foundation ch, **join** *(see Pattern Notes)* in first ch in right hand corner, ch 1, sc in same st as beg ch-1, sc in each of next 9 chs, leaving rem chs unworked, turn. *(10 sc)*

Rows 2–4: Ch 1, sc in each st across, turn.

Row 5: Ch 1, 2 sc in first st, sc in each st across to last st, 2 sc in last st, turn. *(12 sc)*

Row 6: Rep row 2. Fasten off.

2ND LEG
Note: *With RS facing, count 24 worked chs to left of First Leg and mark next st.*

Row 1: With M/N hook and 2 strands of A held tog, join in marked st, ch 1, sc in same st as beg ch-1, sc in each of next 9 chs, leaving rem chs unworked, turn. *(10 sc)*

Rows 2–6: Rep rows 2–6 of First Leg.

Remove marker.

HEAD
Row 1 (RS): With M/N hook and 2 strands of A held tog, join in marked st, ch 1, sc dec in same st as beg ch-1 and next st, sc in each of next 11 sts, 2 sc in last st, turn. *(14 sc)*

Row 2: Ch 1, sc in each st across to last 2 sts, sc dec in last 2 sts, turn. *(13 sc)*

Row 3: Ch 1, sc dec in first 2 sts, sc in each st across to last 2 sts, sc dec in last 2 sts, turn. *(11 sc)*

Row 4: Ch 1, sc in each st across, turn.

Rows 5 & 6: Rep row 3. *(7 sc)*

Row 7: Rep row 4.

Rows 8 & 9: Rep row 3. At end of last row, do not turn or fasten off. *(3 sc)*

EDGING
With RS facing, ch 1, sc evenly sp around piece, working 3 sc in tail corner and each leg corner, join in first sc. Fasten off.

LARGE SPIKE
Row 1 (WS): With M/N hook and 2 strands of B held tog, ch 2, sc in 2nd ch from hook, turn. *(1 sc)*

Row 2: Ch 1, 2 sc in sc, turn. *(2 sc)*

Row 3: Ch 1, sc in each st across, turn.

Row 4: Ch 1, 2 sc in each st across, turn. *(4 sc)*

Row 5: Rep row 3.

Row 6: Ch 1, 2 sc in first sc, sc in each st across to last st, 2 sc in last st, turn. *(6 sc)*

Row 7: Rep row 3.

Rows 8 & 9: Rep row 6. *(10 sc at end of last row)*

Row 10: Rep row 3.

Row 11: Ch 1, sc dec in first 2 sts, sc in each st across to last 2 sts, sc dec in last 2 sts, turn. *(8 sc)*

Row 12: Rep row 3.

Row 13: Ch 1, sc dec in first 2 sts, sc in each st across to last 2 sts, sc dec in last 2 sts, turn. *(6 sc)*

Row 14: Ch 1, sc in each st across. Do not turn.

EDGING
Working across next side, sc in each edge st to point, (sc, ch 2, sc) in point, sc in each edge st to top edge. Do not turn. Do not fasten off.

JOINING
Note: *Mark center 8 sts at top of back.*

Hold Body and Large Spike with WS tog, working through both thicknesses, work 8 sc across marked sts of Back and top edge of Large Spike. Fasten off.

Remove markers.

MEDIUM SPIKE
Make 2.

Rows 1–8: Rep rows 1–8 of Large Spike.

Row 9: Ch 1, sc in each st across, turn.

Row 10: Ch 1, sc dec in first 2 sts, sc in each st across to last 2 sts, sc dec in last 2 sts, turn. *(6 sc)*

Rows 11 & 12: Rep rows 9 and 10. At end of last row, do not turn or fasten off. *(4 sc at end of last row)*

EDGING
Work same as Edging for Large Spike.

JOINING
Note: *With RS facing, count 3 sts to left of Large Spike on Back. Mark this st and each of next 5 sts.*

Join Medium Spike to marked sts in same manner as Large Spike joining, working 6 sc across. Fasten off.

Mark sts on other side of Large Spike in same manner and join 2nd Medium Spike.

Remove markers.

SMALL SPIKE
Make 2.

Row 1 (RS): With M/N hook and 2 strands of B held tog, ch 2, sc in 2nd ch from hook, turn. *(1 sc)*

Rows 2–7: Rep rows 1–7 of Large Spike.

Row 8: Ch 1, sc dec in first 2 sts, sc in each st across to last 2 sts, sc dec in last 2 sts, turn. *(4 sc)*

Row 9: Ch 1, sc in each st across. Do not turn or fasten off.

EDGING
Work same as Edging for Large Spike.

JOINING
Note: *With RS facing, count 3 sts to the left of leftmost Medium Spike on Back, and mark this st and each of next 3 sts.*

Join 4 center sts of Small Spike to marked sts in same manner as joining of Large Spike.

Mark sts on other side of Medium Spike in same manner and join 2nd Small Spike.

Remove markers.

TAIL SPIKES
Make 2.

With M/N hook and 2 strands of B held tog, ch 6, sl st in 2nd ch from hook, sc in next ch, hdc in each of next 3 chs. Do not turn or fasten off.

JOINING
Note: *With RS facing, count 8 sts up from tail corner, mark this st and next st, sk next 2 sts, mark next 2 sts.*

Join Tail Spikes to marked sts in same manner as joining of Large Spike, working 2 sc.

LARGE SPOT
Rnd 1 (RS): With I hook and C, ch 4, join in first ch to form ring, ch 1, 8 sc in ring, join in first sc. *(8 sc)*

Rnd 2: Ch 1, 2 sc in each st around. Leaving long end for sewing, fasten off. *(16 sc)*

SMALL SPOT
Make 2.

With I hook and C, ch 4, join in first ch to form ring, ch 1, 8 sc in ring, join in first sc. Leaving long end for sewing, fasten off. *(8 sc)*

EYE
Make 2.

EYEBALL
With I hook and D, ch 4, join in first ch to form ring, ch 1, 7 sc in ring, join in first sc. Leaving long end for sewing, fasten off. *(7 sc)*

PUPIL
With I hook and E, ch 4, join in first ch to form ring. Leaving long end for sewing, fasten off.

FINISHING
Sew Pupils to Eyeballs with WS together. Referring to photo for placement, sew Eyes to Head and Spots to Body. ∎

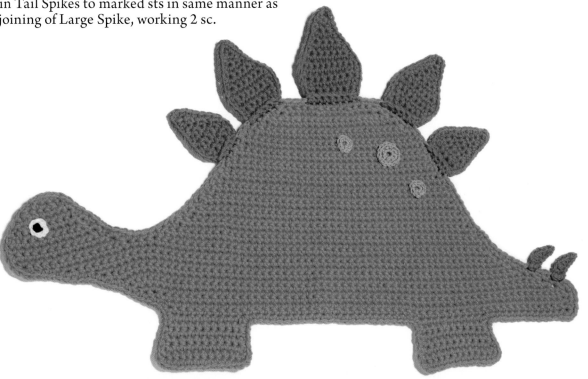

Spots THE LADYBUG

SKILL LEVEL

EASY

FINISHED MEASUREMENTS
32 inches long x 22 inches across ladybug back

MATERIALS
- Deborah Norville Everyday Soft Worsted Solids medium (worsted) weight acrylic yarn (4 oz/203 yds/113g per skein):
    4 skeins #1007 really red (A)
    1 skein each #1012 black (B), #1001 snow white (C) and #1011 chocolate (D)
- Size M/N/13/9mm crochet hook or size needed to obtain gauge
- Size I/9/5.5mm crochet hook
- Tapestry needle
- Stitch markers

GAUGE
Size M/N hook and 2 strands of yarn held tog: 9 sc and 10 rows = 4 inches

PATTERN NOTES
Weave in ends as work progresses.

Chain-2 at beginning of row counts as first double crochet unless otherwise stated.

Join with slip stitch as indicated unless otherwise stated.

BODY
FIRST HALF
Row 1 (RS): With M/N hook and 2 strands of A held tog, ch 60, dc in 3rd ch from hook (*2 sk chs count as first dc*), dc in each rem ch across, turn. (*59 dc*)

Rows 2–5: Ch 2 (*see Pattern Notes*), dc in each st across, turn.

Rows 6–8: Ch 2, **dc dec** (*see Stitch Guide*) in next 2 sts, dc in each st across to last 3 sts, dc dec in next 2 sts, dc in last st. (*53 dc*)

Row 9–12: Ch 2, [dc dec in next 2 sts] twice, dc in each st across to last 5 sts, [dc dec in next 2 sts] twice, dc in last st, turn. (*37 dc*)

Row 13: Ch 2, [dc dec in next 2 sts] 3 times, dc in each st across to last 7 sts, [dc dec in next 2 sts] 3 times, dc in last st. Fasten off. (*31 dc*)

2ND HALF
Row 1 (RS): Hold piece with WS facing and foundation ch at top, working in unused lps on opposite side of foundation ch and with 2 strands of A held tog, **join** (*see Pattern Notes*) in first ch in right-hand corner, ch 2, dc in each rem ch across, turn. (*59 dc*)

Rows 2–13: Rep rows 2–13 of First Half.

EDGING
With RS facing and with M/N hook and 2 strands of A held tog, join in one end of foundation ch, ch 1, sc in same sp as beg ch-1, work 70 sc evenly sp around Half, sc in other end of foundation ch, work 70 sc evenly sp around next Half, join in first sc. Fasten off. (*142 sc*)

HEAD
Note: *With WS facing, count back 8 sts from first st of Edging and mark next st.*

Row 1 (WS): With M/N hook and 2 strands of B held tog, join in marked st, ch 1, sc in same st as beg ch-1, sc in each of next 18 sts, turn. (*19 sc*)

Rows 2–5: Ch 1, sc in each st across, turn.

Rows 6–8: Ch 1, **sc dec** *(see Stitch Guide)* in first 2 sts, sc in each st across to last 2 sts, sc dec in last 2 sts, turn. *(13 sc at end of last row)*

Row 9: Ch 1, sc dec in first 2 sts, sc dec in next 2 sts, sc in each st across to last 4 sts, [sc dec in next 2 sts] twice. Do not turn. *(9 sc)*

Remove marker.

EDGING & LEGS
Ch 1, sc in end of each row down side of Head, sc in each of next 2 sts of Edging, ch 8, sk first 2 chs, hdc in next ch, dc in each of next 5 chs *(leg made)*, sc in each of next 25 sts, ch 8, sk first 2 chs, hdc in next ch, dc in each of next 5 chs *(leg made)*, [sc in each of next 23 sts, ch 8, sk first 2 chs, hdc in next ch, dc in each of the next 5 chs *(leg made)*,] 3 times, sc in each of next 25 sts, ch 8, sk first 2 chs, hdc in next ch, dc in each of the next 5 chs *(leg made)*, sc in each of next 2 sts, sc in end of each row up side of Head, sc in each sc across top of Head, join in first sc. Fasten off.

CENTER STRIPE
With M/N hook and 2 strands of B held tog, ch 65. Fasten off.

SPOTS
Make 4.

Rnd 1 (RS): With I hook and B, ch 4, join in first ch to form ring, ch 1, 7 sc in ring, join in first sc. *(7 sc)*

Rnd 2: Ch 1, 2 sc in each st around, join in first sc. *(14 sc)*

Rnd 3: Ch 1, sc in same st as beg ch-1, 2 sc in next st, *sc in next st, 2 sc in next st, rep from * around, join in first sc. *(21 sc)*

Rnd 4: Ch 1, sc in same st as beg ch-1 and in next st, 2 sc in next st, *sc in each of next 2 sts, 2 sc in next st, rep from * around, join in first sc. *(28 sc)*

Rnd 5: Ch 1, sc in same st as beg ch-1 and in each of next 2 sts, 2 sc in next st, *sc in each of next 3 sts, 2 sc in next st, rep from * around, join in first sc. *(35 sc)*

Rnd 6: Ch 1, sc in same st as beg ch-1 and in each of next 3 sts, 2 sc in next st, *sc in each of next 4 sts, 2 sc in next st, rep from * around, join in first sc. *(42 sc)*

Rnd 7: Ch 1, sc in each st around, join in first sc. Leaving long end for sewing, fasten off.

EYE
Make 2.

EYEBALL

Rnd 1 (RS): With I hook and C, ch 4, join in first ch to form ring, ch 1, 7 sc in ring, join in first sc. *(7 sc)*

Rnd 2: Ch 1, 2 sc in each st around, join in first sc. Leaving long end for sewing, fasten off. *(14 sc)*

PUPIL

With I hook and C, ch 4, join in first ch to form ring, ch 1, 7 sc in ring, join in first sc. Leaving long end for sewing, fasten off. *(7 sc)*

FINISHING

With A, sew Center Stripe down center of Back.

Referring to photo for placement, sew Pupils to center of Eyes. With WS facing, sew Eyes and Spots to Head and Body. ∎

METRIC CONVERSION CHARTS

METRIC CONVERSIONS

yards	x	.9144	=	metres (m)
yards	x	91.44	=	centimetres (cm)
inches	x	2.54	=	centimetres (cm)
inches	x	25.40	=	millimetres (mm)
inches	x	.0254	=	metres (m)

centimetres	x	.3937	=	inches
metres	x	1.0936	=	yards

INCHES INTO MILLIMETRES & CENTIMETRES (Rounded off slightly)

inches	mm	cm	inches	cm	inches	cm	inches	cm
1/8	3	0.3	5	12.5	21	53.5	38	96.5
1/4	6	0.6	5 1/2	14	22	56	39	99
3/8	10	1	6	15	23	58.5	40	101.5
1/2	13	1.3	7	18	24	61	41	104
5/8	15	1.5	8	20.5	25	63.5	42	106.5
3/4	20	2	9	23	26	66	43	109
7/8	22	2.2	10	25.5	27	68.5	44	112
1	25	2.5	11	28	28	71	45	114.5
1 1/4	32	3.2	12	30.5	29	73.5	46	117
1 1/2	38	3.8	13	33	30	76	47	119.5
1 3/4	45	4.5	14	35.5	31	79	48	122
2	50	5	15	38	32	81.5	49	124.5
2 1/2	65	6.5	16	40.5	33	84	50	127
3	75	7.5	17	43	34	86.5		
3 1/2	90	9	18	46	35	89		
4	100	10	19	48.5	36	91.5		
4 1/2	115	11.5	20	51	37	94		

KNITTING NEEDLES CONVERSION CHART

Canada/U.S.	0	1	2	3	4	5	6	7	8	9	10	10½	11	13	15
Metric (mm)	2	2¼	2¾	3¼	3½	3¾	4	4½	5	5½	6	6½	8	9	10

CROCHET HOOKS CONVERSION CHART

Canada/U.S.	1/B	2/C	3/D	4/E	5/F	6/G	8/H	9/I	10/J	10½/K	N
Metric (mm)	2.25	2.75	3.25	3.5	3.75	4.25	5	5.5	6	6.5	9.0

STITCH GUIDE

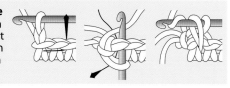

STITCH ABBREVIATIONS

beg	begin/begins/beginning
bpdc	back post double crochet
bpsc	back post single crochet
bptr	back post treble crochet
CC	contrasting color
ch(s)	chain(s)
ch-	refers to chain or space previously made (i.e., ch-1 space)
ch sp(s)	chain space(s)
cl(s)	cluster(s)
cm	centimeter(s)
dc	double crochet (singular/plural)
dc dec	double crochet 2 or more stitches together, as indicated
dec	decrease/decreases/decreasing
dtr	double treble crochet
ext	extended
fpdc	front post double crochet
fpsc	front post single crochet
fptr	front post treble crochet
g	gram(s)
hdc	half double crochet
hdc dec	half double crochet 2 or more stitches together, as indicated
inc	increase/increases/increasing
lp(s)	loop(s)
MC	main color
mm	millimeter(s)
oz	ounce(s)
pc	popcorn(s)
rem	remain/remains/remaining
rep(s)	repeat(s)
rnd(s)	round(s)
RS	right side
sc	single crochet (singular/plural)
sc dec	single crochet 2 or more stitches together, as indicated
sk	skip/skipped/skipping
sl st(s)	slip stitch(es)
sp(s)	space(s)/spaced
st(s)	stitch(es)
tog	together
tr	treble crochet
trtr	triple treble
WS	wrong side
yd(s)	yard(s)
yo	yarn over

YARN CONVERSION

OUNCES TO GRAMS	GRAMS TO OUNCES
1 .... 28.4	25 .... ⅞
2 .... 56.7	40 .... 1⅔
3 .... 85.0	50 .... 1¾
4 .... 113.4	100 .... 3½

UNITED STATES		UNITED KINGDOM
sl st (slip stitch)	=	sc (single crochet)
sc (single crochet)	=	dc (double crochet)
hdc (half double crochet)	=	htr (half treble crochet)
dc (double crochet)	=	tr (treble crochet)
tr (treble crochet)	=	dtr (double treble crochet)
dtr (double treble crochet)	=	ttr (triple treble crochet)
skip	=	miss

Single crochet decrease (sc dec):
(Insert hook, yo, draw lp through) in each of the sts indicated, yo, draw through all lps on hook.

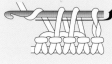

Example of 2-sc dec

Half double crochet decrease (hdc dec):
(Yo, insert hook, yo, draw lp through) in each of the sts indicated, yo, draw through all lps on hook.

Example of 2-hdc dec

Reverse single crochet (reverse sc):
Ch 1, sk first st, working from left to right, insert hook in next st from front to back, draw up lp on hook, yo and draw through both lps on hook.

Chain (ch):
Yo, pull through lp on hook.

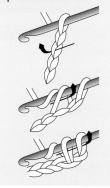

Single crochet (sc):
Insert hook in st, yo, pull through st, yo, pull through both lps on hook.

Double crochet (dc):
Yo, insert hook in st, yo, pull through st, [yo, pull through 2 lps] twice.

Double crochet decrease (dc dec):
(Yo, insert hook, yo, draw lp through, yo, draw through 2 lps on hook) in each of the sts indicated, yo, draw through all lps on hook.

Example of 2-dc dec

Front loop (front lp) Back loop (back lp)

Front Loop   Back Loop

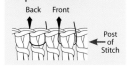

Front post stitch (fp): Back post stitch (bp):
When working post st, insert hook from right to left around post of st on previous row.

Back   Front

Post of Stitch

Half double crochet (hdc):
Yo, insert hook in st, yo, pull through st, yo, pull through all 3 lps on hook.

Double treble crochet (dtr):
Yo 3 times, insert hook in st, yo, pull through st, [yo, pull through 2 lps] 4 times.

Treble crochet decrease (tr dec):
Holding back last lp of each st, tr in each of the sts indicated, yo, pull through all lps on hook.

Example of 2-tr dec

Slip stitch (sl st):
Insert hook in st, pull through both lps on hook.

Chain color change (ch color change)
Yo with new color, draw through last lp on hook.

Double crochet color change (dc color change)
Drop first color, yo with new color, draw through last 2 lps of st.

Treble crochet (tr):
Yo twice, insert hook in st, yo, pull through st, [yo, pull through 2 lps] 3 times.

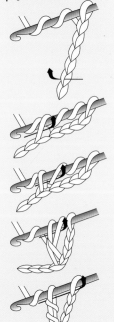

Notes

Cute Crochet Rugs for Kids is published by Annie's, 306 East Parr Road, Berne, IN 46711. Printed in USA. Copyright © 2014 Annie's. All rights reserved. This publication may not be reproduced in part or in whole without written permission from the publisher.

RETAIL STORES: If you would like to carry this pattern book or any other Annie's publication, visit AnniesWSL.com.

Every effort has been made to ensure that the instructions in this pattern book are complete and accurate. We cannot, however, take responsibility for human error, typographical mistakes or variations in individual work. Please visit AnniesCustomerCare.com to check for pattern updates.

ISBN: 978-1-59635-914-7

1 2 3 4 5 6 7 8 9